Ring of Bright Water

Pearson Education Limited
Edinburgh Gate, Harlow,
Essex CM20 2JE, England
and Associated Companies throughout the world.

ISBN-13: 978-0-582-41688-8
ISBN-10: 0-582-41688-4

First published in Great Britain by Longmans Green 1960
First published in the United States of America by E.P. Dutton & Co. Inc. 1961
This adaptation first published by Penguin Books 1998
Publihsed by Addison Wesley Longman Limited and Penguin Books Ltd. 1998
New edition first published 1999

7 9 10 8 6

Original copyright © Gavin Maxwell 1960
Text copyright © J.Y.K. Kerr 1998
Photographs copyright © Gavin Maxwell Enterprises Ltd 1998
Illustrations on pages vi and 2 copyright © Alan Fraser 1998
All rights reserved

All other illustrations reproduced by permission of Gavin Maxwell Enterprises Ltd

Illustrations on pages 4, 7, 9 and 15 are by Peter Scott
The remaining illustrations are by Michael Ayrton on page 21;
Robin McEwen on page 23; and Gavin Maxwell on page 37

Typeset by Digital Type, London
Set in 11/14pt Bembo
Printed in China
SWTC/06

Published by Pearson Education Limited in association with
Penguin Books Ltd, both companies being subsidiaries of Pearson Plc

For a complet list of titles available in the Penguin Readers series please write to your local
Pearson Education office or contact: Penguin Readers Marketing Department,
Pearson Education, Edinburgh Gate, Harlow, Essex, CM20 2JE.

Contents

Introduction

He was my companion for a year and five days and, when he died, it was like losing a child. I now have another otter who is just as beautiful and just as friendly but I know that there will never be another Mijbil.

Gavin Maxwell decides to live alone in a faraway part of the Western Highlands of Scotland. When his much-loved dog, Jonnie, dies, he feels the need for another animal companion.

He chooses an otter. This is the story of three otters that Maxwell looks after: first Chahala, then Mijbil and finally Edal. He tells us about both the trouble and the enjoyment that these unusual animals give him, and about the beautiful natural world round Camusfeàrna, Maxwell's Scottish home.

Maxwell was born in 1914. His family was rich and well-known. He grew up in their large country home in south-west Scotland and it was here that he first became interested in birds and animals. He describes these early years in *The House of Elrig* (1966). He was a soldier and then a businessman before he started to write. He first went to Camusfeàrna in about 1949 and it became his home for nearly twenty years. *Ring of Bright Water* (1960) is the first and most famous of the three books which Maxwell wrote about otters. Maxwell married late in his life and had no children. He died of a serious illness in 1969, at the age of fifty-four.

Camusfeàrna caught fire and burned down the year before Gavin Maxwell died, and today nothing is left of the house. Edal the otter died in the fire.

Chapter 1   How I First Came to Camusfeàrna

I am writing this in my kitchen, which is also my sitting-room. On the sofa there is an otter, asleep on its back with its front legs in the air. Outside the open door, across the grass, there is the beach. I can hear the waves of the sea as they break on it. Through the window a group of wild geese fly past. They land on the grassy field beside the house. I can hear their quiet talk as they walk about. I can hear the sounds of the geese and the sound of the sea and the deep crashing sound of the waterfall. These are the only things that I can hear in the stillness round me.

All round my house there are mountains: mountains, islands and the sea. There are very few people. The nearest house to mine is called Druimfiaclach. It's high above me, about a mile up the mountainside, where the road is. There's no road to my house: you have to walk. The nearest village is about eight kilometres away.

This place has been my home for ten years now. I know every tree and every stone of it. I have lived in many places but I shall always come back here to the things that I know and love, as long as I live. The name of my home is Camusfeàrna.

What am I doing here, at this kitchen table? What brought me to this beautiful part of Scotland, to live so far from other people? I'll start from the beginning. I was born in the south of Scotland and grew up there. My family lived in a big house in the country and that's how I became interested in birds and animals. At the end of the Second World War, I decided to start a sea-fishing business on an island called Soay in the west of Scotland. I worked very hard to build up the business but it never made much money. In the end I sold it and went to live in London. I tried to make money by painting pictures of people

1

but I was never really happy. One day I met a friend from my years at university and I told him about my troubles.

'I've just bought some land in Scotland, in the West Highlands,' he told me. 'There's a small house on part of the land. It's on the coast and miles from anywhere. It's standing empty, because none of the local people wants to live there. There's no road to it and it's too far from the nearest village. You're welcome to have it if you'll look after it for me. Are you interested?'

I didn't have to think twice. 'I'm very interested,' I answered. I knew in my heart that this was the place for me. My friend gave me the door-key and a few days later I took the car and drove to Scotland, about eight hundred kilometres north.

The journey was long and tiring. As I went towards the North, the country got wilder, the mountains bigger and the villages fewer. For the last sixty kilometres the road became very narrow – too narrow for two cars to get past at the same time. Finally I came to a small house called Druimfiaclach, the home of the MacKinnon family. They are my nearest neighbours and my very dear friends but I didn't know them then. I was not alone on this journey: my much-loved dog Jonnie was with me. He was an old dog now but he still went with me everywhere. Together we began to make our way down the mountain. From the road you can't see the coastline below but I followed the stream that cuts into the side of the mountain, turning as it goes. Jonnie ran in front of me.

Sometimes the stream fell straight down into a dark pool, then ran quietly among rocks, then fell again. It was early spring. The small trees growing along the stream still had no leaves but there were beautiful yellow flowers in the grass near the water. The wind was cold and the tops of the mountains were white with snow but the sky was cloudless and bright blue. The stream became narrower. We turned a corner and suddenly we could see below us the sea and the line of the coast and Camusfeàrna.

The house stood in a wide grassy field that was almost an island because the stream makes a half-circle round it before it runs into the sea. A few sheep were eating the grass near the house. Past the field I could see a beautiful white beach with rocks at each end and after the beach was the sea. In the sea there was a group of little islands lying in a line about half a mile long. Far away across the sea I could see the island of Skye with its wonderful mountains and valleys, blue-grey in the sunlight. At the side of the field there were two other stone buildings without roofs, one of them very near the water. But my eyes were on Camusfeàrna, a house with glass in its windows and a roof on its walls. I began to walk faster. At the bottom of the mountain the stream became wider as it ran past the field to meet the sea. Jonnie and I crossed it and a minute later I turned the key in the door of my new home for the very first time.

The geese fly over Camusfeàrna

Chapter 2   My Only Neighbours

Inside the house there wasn't a single piece of furniture. There was no running water and no electric light. The air was cold – colder than the air outside. But to me Camusfeàrna was perfection. The house was bigger than I thought. On the ground floor there was a sitting-room and a kitchen, with a little back kitchen also. Upstairs there were two more rooms. The inside walls were made of wood. I had some bedding with me, some tins of food and something to cook the food with. I knew that I could easily make other pieces of furniture from fish-boxes, which you can find on every beach in the west of Scotland. In those early days of living at Camusfeàrna, I used these boxes to make chairs and tables, putting towels over them to hide the wood underneath. Even today the house is full of furniture made of fish-boxes: for example, the sofa in the sitting-room and the clothes cupboards in my bedroom. After living here for ten years, I also know that nearly everything that you need in a house washes up on the beach sooner or later – all you have to do is wait.

But in those first weeks I decided that I needed to buy a few pieces of furniture. It wasn't easy because the nearest railway station was over a hundred and sixty kilometres away. In the end I drove to the hotel at Lochailort, which had some furniture that the hotel-keeper didn't want: badly made and really ugly things. I bought a bed, two kitchen tables, three hard wooden chairs and something to put on the floor. These pieces came first by train and then by boat and it cost me a lot of money to bring them. After that I decided not to buy anything more. In the following months friends who came to stay helped me to make more furniture from the wood that we picked up on the beaches along the coast. It has taken a long time to make these cold, empty rooms into a real home but the house is now the most

The sitting-room at Camusfeàrna

comfortable house that I know, and my visitors seem to think the same.

In Britain it is unusual to go to sleep knowing that there are no other people nearer than two kilometres and that this one family is the only one for eight kilometres more. This feeling of being quite alone is strangely exciting. I think that I notice the natural world round me much more because there are so few people.

That first night I lay in bed listening to the sounds of the night: the feet of small animals running behind the house, the cry of the seabirds waiting for the sea to go out and, further away, the crash of the waterfall. The sound of the waterfall is in your ears day and night. In winter the sound is loud and deep, in summer it's softer but it's a sound that never stops. When I'm away from

Camusfeàrna and remember the place, it's always the waterfall that I think of first. These were the noises that came to my ears that first night as I rested my head against Jonnie's warm side and slept.

♦

I haven't yet said much about my neighbours, the MacKinnons. Calum Murdo MacKinnon is a man of about forty, and the local road-mender. I was surprised to find that he reads lots of newspapers and books and that he's full of information on all kinds of subjects. I've learned a lot of things from him that I didn't know before. Morag is Calum Murdo's wife. She's a good-looking woman, who has a great love of birds and animals. Wild swans come for a few weeks every winter to the little lake across the road from the MacKinnons' house. Morag loves the swans and they seem to know this. Every time she opens her front door, the swans call to her across the lake and she calls back to them.

The MacKinnons have three sons. The oldest boy, Lachlan, was thirteen when I first arrived. His two brothers, Ewan and Donald, were eleven years old. The younger boys were very helpful to me. They often brought letters down to me in the evenings after school. At weekends they did jobs for me about the house. For

The wild swans

example, with the help of an old ladder they painted the outside walls of the house for me, leaving it a beautiful snowy white.

As time went by, all the things that I needed from the outside world came through the MacKinnons: letters, shopping, information. The nearest village with more than one shop is fifty kilometres away. Letters come from this shopping centre by boat to a small village eight kilometres away and from there the postman carries them in his car to the different addresses in the neighbourhood. Newspapers get to me two days late. The mountains round about are so high that it's very difficult to hear programmes on the radio. Shopping is also quite difficult. I leave my order for food and other things at Druimfiaclach and next morning the postman takes it to the man with the boat, who takes it to the right shop in the 'shopping centre' and brings back the things that I've asked for. There are a surprising number of shops for a small village but the problem is that the shops have very little in them. If I want to buy, for example, a pair of blue jeans, the nearest place that sells them is Inverness, nearly a hundred and sixty kilometres away on the eastern coast of Scotland. Sometimes I've asked for something like oil for a lamp and the shopkeeper, not having any oil, has sent me a kilo of sausages instead!

Chapter 3   Companions

Eight years after I first came to Camusfeàrna, I was able to bring running water to the house. Until then, I had to get water from the stream. I took it from a place near the crossing, where the water was very clean. One winter there was so much rain that the stream became a river and broke up the wooden crossing, carrying the pieces out to sea. After that I used a line as a way of getting across the stream but it wasn't very safe.

For a time I had four of Morag's goats as my companions and

Three of Morag's goats

I was able to enjoy goat's milk for breakfast. Goats eat anything and once or twice I came home from an afternoon's fishing to find one of them in my kitchen, finishing my bread or my potatoes. Then one day they ate the leaves of a poisonous plant, which killed them.

I caught and ate a lot of fish and other kinds of seafood. At first I did not have a boat because I couldn't find a place with deep water near the beach. Now I have two boats and I can move up or down the coast when I want. But storms blow up very suddenly in the West Highlands. In a minute or two, smooth blue water becomes great angry waves and the wind drives small boats like mine onto the rocks. Sailing here can be a dangerous business.

Every year something very strange happens. The mouth of the stream is full of baby eels, making their way up the stream from the sea. There are millions of them, each one eight centimetres long, born two thousand miles away across the Atlantic Ocean and moving to new homes in fresh water all over Scotland. Many die and many more become the food of seabirds; but some are able to climb over the rocks and get past all the waterfalls. It's a mystery how they do it but I have seen them in rivers six hundred metres above the sea.

I remember another time one warm September when the MacKinnon boys came down to Camusfeàrna for an evening swim. I was inside the house reading when I heard shouts of excitement from the beach. The boys were standing up to their knees in the calm sea, shouting and laughing and throwing water about. The water was thick with little silver fish – thousands and thousands of them. Soon they even began to throw themselves out of the water and onto the beach. It was only later that I understood why. Out at sea a large number of bigger fish were following the small ones, eating as many as they could. For the next few days Jonnie and I ate all the fish that we wanted and more, until we were tired of them.

But my much loved companion was getting old. He was happier in the country than in London, so I left him with Morag one winter, while I went south. She telephoned to say that he was ill. I travelled back to Camusfeàrna and sat with him for many nights until he got better. Sadly, he didn't stay healthy for long: a second, even more serious illness began. I remembered him as a young dog when we went out shooting together, bringing back each dead bird that I shot in his mouth. Now he was so weak that he couldn't stand up. He could only move his tail a little when I came into the room. Once again I had to go to London. Morag wrote to me, saying that there was no hope for Jonnie and asking me to give my agreement to the doctor, who then put Jonnie to sleep. He died in Morag's arms, because I wasn't brave enough to be there.

Chapter 4   Chahala

After Jonnie died, I knew that I didn't want another dog. But during the autumn and winter days at Camusfeàrna with their long hours of darkness I felt very alone. I remember the wet firewood that didn't burn and the wet clothes that never dried. I wanted an animal companion to live with me but I could not decide which animal to choose. I put the idea to one side and for a year I thought no more about it.

Early in 1956, I went with my friend Wilfred Thesiger to live for two months among the Marsh Arabs of Southern Iraq. While I was there, I had the idea of keeping an otter instead of a dog. Camusfeàrna, with both fresh and salt water, seemed the perfect place for an otter to live in. I talked about my idea with Wilfred at the beginning of our journey.

'Get one while you are in the Marshes,' he told me. 'There are lots of them here. Many of the Arabs keep otters in their homes.'

One evening we were sitting in the home of an Arab friend, listening to the men's conversation. Suddenly I heard the Arabic word for otter: 'water dog'.

'What are they saying about otters?' I asked Thesiger, who understood Arabic very well.

'This man is from the next village. He says that he's got a young otter at home. It's very small and still drinks milk from a bottle. Do you want it?'

Of course I said yes. The man went away to bring the otter. He soon came back with the animal in his arms and put it down on my knee. She was a female, the size of a little cat, with a tail as long as a pencil. She turned over onto her back, showing her round stomach and four little feet, without any shyness. I immediately asked to buy her. In the end, after a lot of talking, we agreed on a price of five dinars and we also bought the baby's bottle – something not easy to find in that part of the world. I tied her to my wrist to stop her from running away. Then I put her inside my shirt, a warm dark place where she felt comfortable. I carried her everywhere like this. When she was awake, she liked to put her head out through the top of my pullover. Usually her call was like a little bird but in her sleep she

Camusfeàrna

*Jonnie above
Camusfeàrna*

had a different cry, which seemed sad. I named her Chahala, which was the name of the river where we bought her. Also, the name had the same sound as her sleeping cry.

From the beginning Chahala was very clean. She went outside for her toilet needs and then she climbed up onto my shoulder, very pleased with herself, and asked softly for her bottle of milk. She liked to drink it lying on her back, with the bottle between her front legs. When she finished, she often fell asleep with the bottle still in her mouth, looking perfectly happy. From the beginning, she thought of me as her parent but unluckily I did not know all the things that a real parent must know. We went for walks together and when she was tired of walking, she touched my legs and gave her bird-like cry until I picked her up. Then she jumped inside my pullover and often fell asleep head down with her tail coming out against my face. The Arabs were very amused by this and called her my daughter.

I decided to give her food to eat instead of milk. I killed two small birds and was planning to mix some of their blood in her bottle of milk. But as soon as Chahala saw the red meat, she wanted to eat it. I gave her the meat cut into small pieces and she ate it greedily. 'No more milk,' the Arab boat-boy said. 'Only meat from now.' But suddenly everything went wrong. A week later, we shot a big river bird. I gave small pieces of the bird's meat to Chahala. I did not realize that this was her last meal. That night she was restless and moved about continuously inside my sleeping bag. In the morning I could see that she was very ill. Soon I understood that she was dying. We gave her some oil but it didn't help her. She lay face down in the boat, her body shaking. When I picked her up, she suddenly became soft in my hands and stopped moving. 'She's dead,' I said in Arabic, so that the boat-boys could understand. They sat quite still, hoping that it was not true. 'Are you sure?' said Thesiger. I gave him Chahala's body. 'Yes,' he said. 'She's dead.' He threw the body into the water.

It landed in a bed of white and yellow flowers. She lay on her back, just the way she liked to sleep when she was alive. Slowly the boat moved on but the boat-boys went on looking at her until she was too far away to see. The sun shone on the river and I felt terribly unhappy; but now I knew the answer to my problem. The animal companion that I wanted to have at Camusfeàrna was an otter.

Later I learned why Chahala died. The Arabs often use a special poison to catch fish. The river bird which we shot ate fish and probably had poison in its body. It was not strong enough to kill the bird but it was too strong for a baby otter.

It was time for Wilfred and I to leave the river country. We went to spend a few days in the town of Basra before the next part of our journey. Chahala's dying seemed like the end of something but in fact it was a beginning.

Chapter 5   Another Otter

In Basra we stayed with a British friend. Wilfred left again after two days but I stayed longer, waiting for letters from England. One afternoon the letters came. I was just starting to read them when two Arabs arrived. One of them had a bag with some sort of animal in it. They gave me a letter from Thesiger. 'Here is your otter,' it said. 'It's a male and it already eats meat. You'll probably want to take it to London. Please tell me that it has arrived safely.'

When the Arabs opened the bag and I saw the animal inside, I fell in love with a love which, all these years later, is still alive in me. The otter which came out was a chocolate brown colour and his coat was dirty but beautifully soft. I could see that he was of a type very different from Chahala, and in fact I learned later that he was a kind of otter which people didn't know about until then. I called him Mijbil, which was the name of one of my Iraqi

Arab friends. He was my companion for a year and five days and when he died, it was like losing a child. I now have another otter who is just as beautiful and just as friendly but I know that there will never be another Mijbil.

At first Mijbil was not very interested in me. He chose to sleep on the floor as far from my bed as possible. He did not eat or drink much. In fact his food was a problem. I was afraid to give him fish from the market which perhaps had in them the same poison that killed Chahala. I was able to find a fisherman who sold me fish that were still alive and Mijbil ate these with great enjoyment.

I stayed with my British friend for two weeks. The second night Mijbil climbed onto my bed in the darkness and lay against the back of my knees. He soon began to be interested in everything around him – much too interested, in fact. I made a sort of leather harness for him and took him with me on a lead to the bathroom. He loved his bath and swam up and down, throwing water everywhere. Two days later he escaped from my bedroom and went straight to the bathroom alone. In a minute

Mijbil

15

he taught himself how to turn on the water and I now realized that this animal was very intelligent. We spent part of each day in my friend's walled garden. Mijbil soon began to follow me and to come when I called his name. I found that he loved playing games. I gave him a rubber ball and he pushed it along with his feet like a footballer or used his shoulder to throw it in the air. He also liked small glass balls. He lay on his back and moved them up and down between his front feet without ever dropping them on the ground. I began to understand Mij's language: the cries and calls that he used to show how he felt. His teeth were terribly strong but during all the time we were together he only once bit me.

The days went by pleasantly in Basra but I was deeply worried about flying to London with Mij. He had to travel in a wooden box not more than fifty centimetres long, which had to stay at my feet during the journey. Mij's body was already about thirty centimetres long, not counting his tail, so in a box that size he could move very little. Another problem was that we had to change planes in Paris. When the day came for us to leave, I had the box ready. It was made of wood, with metal on the inside to make it stronger and holes in the top to give him air. I decided to put him in his box an hour before we left and he seemed quite calm when I went for my evening meal. When I came back, there was blood coming out of the air-holes. Frightened, I opened the box to find the metal inside all torn away. Mij's mouth, nose and feet had cuts on them. He gave a sad cry and tried to climb up my leg. There was very little time: the plane was leaving in half an hour and we were eight kilometres away. I pulled out all the metal and with a heavy heart put Mij back in his box. The driver drove like the wind. Just as we arrived, I heard the sound of breaking wood and Mij's nose was coming out of the box. I ran to the aeroplane, holding the two halves of the box together.

Luckily my place was right at the front, next to a well-dressed

Mijbil wearing his harness

American woman. I took out some old newspapers and put them on the floor. I gave a packet of fish to the young woman who was looking after the passengers and asked her to keep it in the fridge. Of course Mij soon escaped from his box and ran away under the passengers' chairs. I could hear someone screaming 'A rat! A rat!' but the young woman immediately went to talk to her and she became calm again. I got up to search for Mij but the girl said sweetly: 'Please stay in your place. I will find him and bring him to you.' Just when I was beginning to lose hope, Mij jumped onto my knee and began kissing my face and neck. I was the only person on the plane that he knew and felt comfortable with; from that night on, we were friends for ever.

For the next hour or two he slept on top of me. When he woke up, I asked for fish and water. Mijbil tore up the newspapers and took all the things out of the American woman's bag while she was sleeping. Luckily I was able to put them back before she woke up. Just before we landed at Paris, I had to put Mij back in his box. It hurt me to do this but there was no other way. I tied the two halves of the box together as well as I could. Mij began to cry again but after some minutes he was silent. Later, I found that he went into a very deep sleep, something that some animals do if they feel that they are in danger. From Paris the aeroplane took us not to London but to Amsterdam. We waited there for hours but finally we got to London. A car was waiting for us. As soon as I got to my flat, I opened the box and Mij jumped into my arms, wonderfully happy to be safe and free.

Chapter 6   Mijbil in London

At that time I was living in a flat in London which had a big sitting-room and an upstairs bedroom. At the back there was a small kitchen, a bathroom and a room for keeping bags and boxes in. There was no garden but instead there was a door opening onto the garage roof, so Mij could go outside when he wanted. If I put him in the box-room, he could also use the bathroom. I was able to leave Mij alone like this for a few hours but never more than four or five at the most. Otters need a lot of love and someone to play with. Without these things they quickly become unhappy and angry, and start to make trouble.

That first morning in London, Mijbil wanted to see and touch everything in the flat. There was fish for him to eat and after that he had a wonderful time swimming in the bath for half an hour. I was terribly tired, so I put a sleeping bag on the sofa and got inside it. Immediately Mij climbed onto the sofa, got into the bag beside me and lay flat on his back with his front legs in the air. In a minute he was fast asleep.

Mij and I stayed in London for nearly a month. I built a wall round the garage roof and made a door on the stairs to my bedroom, so that I could keep him out of the sitting-room if I needed to. I put the telephone inside a box, which he quickly learned to open. If a visitor came, I sometimes put Mij in the bedroom but he didn't like that and usually began to tear or break things until he was free again. He often played with his little balls of glass or rubber, sometimes throwing them right across the room. I had a broken suitcase, which stood against a chair. Mij loved to drop one of his balls at the top end, watch it run down to the bottom and then catch it again. These games kept him happy for about half the time that he spent in the flat but he wanted to spend the other half playing with me. He liked to hide behind an armchair and then run out if a foot came near him; or he jumped about excitedly like a young dog, giving playful little bites with his strong teeth. Sometimes I took a towel and tied one of his playthings inside it. Mij then had to use his feet and teeth to open the towel, which he was able to do in five or ten minutes. When he finished, he looked up, waiting for me to say 'Well done!' At night he slept in my bed and every morning we had a bath together. Outside the house I put him on his lead and took him for walks, just like a dog. He loved to smell the smells that were left by dogs but if we met one, I picked him up immediately because I was afraid of a fight.

About this time Mij gave me a serious bite. It happened like this. Every day I gave him eels to eat, a food that all otters love. I kept the eels in a big pot of water in the kitchen and gave them to him in the bath. If he got too excited, I shut him in the bathroom with three or four eels until he became quieter. One day I forgot to shut the bathroom door and Mij came into the sitting-room carrying an eel in his mouth. It's always dangerous to take food away from an animal, so I did nothing. But then he decided to take his eel to the bedroom. I knew that he was

19

planning to eat it in my bed. This was too much. I quickly put on three pairs of thick gloves and caught him half-way up the stairs. He put the eel down and made a kind of singing noise. When I put my hand on the eel, the noise got louder. Then when I picked it up, he bit me. His teeth went through all three gloves and met in the middle of my hand. Mij immediately seemed very unhappy. When I carried the eel to the bath, he now didn't want it. 'Did I hurt you?' he seemed to say. 'I'm so sorry.' His bite made a deep hole in my hand, which was soon the size of a football and took a week or two to get better.

I wanted to know more about the different kinds of otter, so I went to the Natural History Museum. I invited Mr Hayman, who worked there, to come and look at Mijbil at my flat. He studied Mij's shape, colour and teeth very carefully. Later I was surprised to learn that Mijbil was a new kind of otter, for which there was no name. So they named this new kind of otter after me, calling it Maxwell's Otter, which pleased me greatly.

♦

It was now early May, and I very much wanted to take Mij to Camusfeàrna. I knew that his true home was there, not in a London flat. Travelling with an otter is an expensive business. This time we went by train but I didn't want to put Mij in a box again. I bought a dog-ticket for him and a sleeping-car ticket for myself. In this way we were able to travel together and without other people. On the way I stopped to visit my family at Monreith, in the south of Scotland. Here Mij was able to swim freely for the first time: first on the big lake near my family's home and then in the sea. I made a little body-harness for him out of pieces of leather. I tied a lead to the harness if I didn't want him to go too far away. But the harness was important also because it showed that Mij was not a wild animal. We went on many walks together. He was no more trouble than a dog and

Mij swimming

much more interesting to watch. Mij loved to be near any piece of open water. He taught himself to catch things to eat: sometimes an eel, more often frogs. Luckily he was not interested in chickens. Even in the country he liked brightly coloured things and kept them to play with, often carrying them for miles: a flower, a round stone or a woman's handkerchief, which he found one day by the roadside. I was surprised that the smells left by other otters didn't interest him: there were many in the streams and rivers round us. Mij only once killed a warm-blooded animal and even then he didn't eat it. He found a baby bird and, thinking this was another toy, he put it under his arm while he went swimming. Of course the little bird couldn't breathe and died under the water. After Mij returned to dry land, he was surprised that the bird didn't move when he tried to play with it. In the end he got bored and left it where it lay.

Chapter 7   Camusfeàrna Again

We finally arrived at Camusfeàrna in early June. We had several weeks of really hot weather. When I think about early summer there, I remember the wild roses – deep pink ones – wonderful to look at against the bright blue sea. Mij immediately made himself at home. The waterfall, the stream, the beach, the little islands: he was in all those places every day and never stopped enjoying himself. He always returned to the house at night, or in the daytime if he felt tired.

M: in my bed as before but now he preferred to sleep
        othes, with his nose pointing at my feet. Every
        at the same time: twenty minutes past eight. I
        s soon as he was awake, he came to press his
        vith little loving cries. If I didn't get up
        to get me out of bed. First he undid all the

Camusfeàrna

bedclothes and then pulled them off the bed onto the floor. I sleep without anything on, so I soon began to feel cold. I had to get up and get dressed. Mij sat watching me, pleased that he was getting what he wanted.

Next, Mij went off to the eel-box in the stream and had his breakfast. Then he played in the stream and the sea, swimming after fish in the deep pools, turning over stones in the hope of finding eels, then throwing himself into the waves to look for more fish that were hiding on the sea floor. Finally he came back to the house to dry himself among his towels. For the first two weeks I stayed with him until he got tired but after that I went back to the house when he finished his breakfast. As time went on, he stayed fishing or playing by the stream for hours and I only began to worry if he didn't come home by midday.

There were cows in the field that summer and they often came to drink at the stream. Mij thought of a new game. He liked to come up quietly behind a cow while it was drinking and pull its tail. Then he jumped back to escape the dangerous kicks of the cow. Mij found this game very amusing and never got hurt.

That summer I was writing a book and I lay for hours in the sun near the waterfall. From time to time Mij jumped out of the water and ran up to me to say hello, welcoming me like a long-lost friend. One of the problems of living with an otter is the way it likes to get dry after swimming. It lies on its back and pushes itself against you until its skin is dry and you are very wet. I learned to keep my bedroom door closed, to stop Mij from drying himself on my bed; but the pages that I was writing got very wet because of Mij's visits. Sometimes he even took my pen with him when he left for another swim.

Mij was a wonderful swimmer, at his best in deep water. He could stay under the water for as long as six minutes without coming up for air. If I was in a boat, he liked to swim near it. His head came up out of the water first on one side, then on the other. Sometimes he climbed into the boat to dry himself and give me a shower-bath in the usual way. July was the season for mackerel, a kind of fish. Mij loved to eat them but he didn't catch them for himself. He was good at catching other kinds of fish, specially eels. The eels often hid under stones at the bottom of a stream. If a stone was too big for Mij to lift, he called me to come and lift it for him. When the eel swam out from under the stone, Mij went racing after it like a bullet from a gun.

I never asked Mijbil to give me a fish as a present but one day he did. At first I thought that he just wanted to show it to me, so I said: 'Very good, Mij' and walked away. But Mij followed me and again put the dead fish at my feet. This time I picked it up carefully – I didn't want another bite – and made the movements of eating it. This made him happy and he threw himself head-first back into the sea.

I worried about Mij when the sea was rough and at those times I tried to keep him away from rocks. Once he was sitting on a rock eating a fish. A very big wave came up and crashed down on top of him. When the water fell back off the rocks, I

The coast near Camusfeàrna

was afraid of seeing his dead body but to my surprise he was still in the same place, calmly eating his fish. Mij loved the waves. He liked to throw himself into each big grey wall of water and swim right through it. He swam through wave after wave until all I could see was a little black head far out to sea. At times like those I thought that he was gone, never to return.

As time went on, Mij stayed away from the house longer and longer. This worried me and I often searched for him for hours. Once he went up above the waterfall to the part of the stream where it runs between high rocks. He was away for about nine hours and I looked for him everywhere. The noise of the water was very loud, so he couldn't hear me when I called and I couldn't hear his cries. Finally I found him on a flat piece of rock too small for him to go on his way or turn back. Below him the water fell straight down for about fifteen metres. My heart was in my mouth but somehow I was able to climb down and save him. He was frightened and very hungry but also very glad to be in my arms again.

Another time Mij stayed away all day and all night. Again I searched the stream and the beach and the ground all round the house. Finally I found an otter's footprints on the beach. I didn't know if these were Mij's footprints or those of a wild otter but I had the idea that he was on one of the islands. It was a stormy night and the sea was very rough. When it began to get light, I decided to take my little boat and search for him there. Waves were coming into the boat and I was in danger of running onto the rocks, because of the strong wind. I looked all over the island but I couldn't find Mij anywhere. With a heavy heart I went back home. All that day I walked about calling Mij's name. I began to understand that this young animal was of great importance to me. By the evening I was sure that he was dead. Sadly I took away his drinking dish from under the kitchen table and then went to throw away his half-finished plate of rice and egg. Just then I thought that I heard the 'Hah?' sound which Mij always made when he came into an empty room. I walked to the door and called his name but all was quiet. As I went back to the kitchen, I saw a large wet footprint of an otter on the floor. I thought I was seeing something that wasn't really there. I got down on my knees to look more carefully. Then I heard the sound 'Hah?' again and this time I knew that there was no mistake. Suddenly Mij was dancing all round me, jumping all over me, climbing on my back and calling out in great excitement, so happy to be home again. It was only then that I noticed his harness, which was badly torn. I realized that the harness probably got caught on some piece of wood and metal and that Mij was a prisoner for hours, until he was able to bite through the leather and get free.

Mij loved to take his playthings into the stream and play games with them there. Sometimes he brought a table-tennis ball from the house, pushing it under the water and watching it jump up, catching it and letting it go again. One day I tried to take some photographs of him while he played with his ball like this. I put my foot in the wrong place and fell into the water beside him, still holding the camera. I was on my way back to change my wet clothes when I heard a call. It was a visitor, a woman who was also a well-known writer. There's a stone wall which goes from the waterfall to the house and we began talking across the top of the wall. Mij loved to meet new people and climbed onto the wall next to me. My visitor rested her arm on the wall as she talked, her head quite near Mij. Just then, Mij suddenly jumped up and bit the woman's ear. She made no movement and went on talking as usual; but when I looked at her face, I could see that she was both very surprised and terribly angry. It is a mystery that she and I are still quite good friends.

Chapter 8 How Mijbil Died

Mij and I went back to London in the autumn. He seemed quite pleased to be back in the London flat and our usual games began again: eels in the bath, walks on a lead through the dirty London streets, even an afternoon of shopping. But there was still a serious problem. I couldn't leave Mij alone for more than four or five hours. I was planning to visit another country and I needed to find someone to look after Mij while I was away. But first, in November, I had to be away on business in the north of England for three days. The London Zoo agreed to take him and give him a room in their hospital. Mij did not like to see me go. I telephoned from the north the next day to ask if he was all right. They told me that Mij wasn't eating any food and that he was now in a very deep sleep. They told me to come for him as soon as possible, because it's easy for animals to die when they stay sleeping like this for a long time. I drove back to London as fast as I could. When I arrived at the animal hospital and went to Mij's room, I couldn't see him anywhere. He was still asleep inside an old jacket which I had left there for him. I put my hand inside the jacket and felt his warm body. Slowly he began to wake up and then he climbed out, wonderfully pleased to see me. It was clear that the animal hospital was not the answer to my problem: I couldn't possibly leave Mij there again.

I started looking for someone to be Mij's keeper at times when I was away from home: anything from one or two days to several months. I saw about forty people who wanted the job but I still couldn't find the right person. Some didn't have suitable homes, others were much too young. Few of them had any idea of the difficulties of being the keeper of an otter. After two months things were no better. I decided to go back to Camusfeàrna in the spring and write a book about Mij. This plan left me more time to find the person that I needed.

I have now come to the last part of Mij's story. I shall tell it quickly because when I remember those terrible days, I still feel deeply unhappy. I wanted to leave London in early April but I had to have two weeks without Mij to visit libraries and do other important business. A friend agreed to take Mij to Scotland and look after him at Camusfeàrna for those two weeks. So I packed up all the things that Mij needed: harnesses, leads, a special kind of rice, his favourite playthings, and went with them both to the railway station to say goodbye. I remember Mij well – he was playing with my pen as we sat in the taxi and his coat shone under the bright electric lights. He got into the train and clearly felt at home in the sleeping car. We said goodbye. It was the last time that I saw him.

During the next ten days I got several letters from my friend telling me about Mij. He was happy to be back at Camusfeàrna. He swam, he caught fish and, when he was tired, he came in and lay in front of the fire. He often disappeared for many hours, which worried my friend. He took Mij's leather harness off because he thought Mij was safer without it.

On 16th April I packed my bags. I was planning to be at Camusfeàrna the following afternoon when I got a telephone call from someone who lived in the neighbourhood. 'I've heard a story about a man who's just killed an otter at a village eight kilometres north of Camusfeàrna,' he told me. 'I don't know if the otter was yours but I understand that your animal has disappeared.' There was no more information.

I immediately drove north and arrived at the village the following day. Different people had different stories to tell. Some said that the dead otter was a wild one and very old. I knew this wasn't true. I knew that Mij was dead but I needed to know who killed him and how and why. It was a workman called Big Angus, people said. He was driving along in his lorry when he saw an otter on the road near the sea. He killed it but didn't keep the dead body. I asked where Angus lived and drove to his house. When he got home from work, I asked him to show me the place of the killing.

'I saw the animal here at the side of the road,' he said. 'I took a tool from the back of the lorry and killed him with it. This wasn't your otter because he was very old and thin. I threw the body into the river. I don't remember where I threw it.'

Of course I pressed him to tell me the true story but he had nothing more to say. Later, another man in the village came to see me. 'Angus is lying,' he said. 'I saw the animal's body on the lorry when it stopped in the village. It was young, not old, with a beautiful skin. Only the head was badly broken. A wild otter will not sit waiting for you to kill it, like this one did. Angus just wants to keep out of trouble.'

My friend told me more about what happened. During those two weeks Mij made several long journeys up and down the coast. One day he was in a village twelve kilometres to the south. Several people saw him but they left him alone. The next time, he went north up the coast to a different village. He was going back home when he met Big Angus. Unlike a wild otter, Mij was not afraid of people and that was one of the reasons why he died. He and I were together for just a year and five days up until the night that he left London. It was so short a time.

Chapter 9 'What a Piece of Luck!'

I felt terribly sad about losing Mij and very alone without him. He was so much a part of Camusfeàrna that I had to wait for a full year before I felt able to go back there. Instead of staying in Scotland, I went to Italy to finish some writing work that I started there a long time before. As the long summer months went by under the burning Italian sun, Camusfeàrna at times

30

seemed quite unreal. When I returned to London, I moved to a new flat. In the old one I was thinking too much about the past. I tried keeping two other animals as companions but the first was dangerous and the second was boring. I then tried keeping small birds but they were not the answer. In March of the following year I decided to go back to Camusfeàrna. It was my real home but again I felt the emptiness that I knew when Mij died. Slowly I realized that I could not go on living alone at Camusfeàrna: I had to have another otter.

I wrote to all the animal-lovers that I knew, asking for their help. I asked up and down the coast about wild otter families. I tried to get another otter from the Marshes of Iraq. I agreed to buy an otter from India but it died on the journey to Britain. These plans took up a lot of time, and needed lots of letters and telephone calls but they all came to nothing. I even found an otter-keeper: a young boy of fifteen called Jimmy Watt, who loved animals and wanted to work with them, but still I had no otter.

Then something very strange and wonderful happened. On 19th April I drove to the railway station fifty kilometres from Camusfeàrna to meet a friend. He often came to stay with me and was one of those people who made a lot of the furniture that I've got in my house. I arrived in the village early, to do some shopping and to have lunch in the hotel. I met my friend and we came back to the hotel for a drink. We were sitting and talking in the sun-room which looks out over the sea. Suddenly the doorman of the hotel, an old friend of mine, came running in.

'Mr Maxwell, Mr Maxwell! Come quickly and see this strange animal outside. Quick, now!'

I went to the front door. Four people were walking past the hotel towards a parked car near the water. Behind them walked a large otter with a smooth skin and a beautiful white throat. It all seemed quite unreal. I went up to the group and began telling them excitedly all about Mijbil and how I was looking for another otter to take his place. They told me about their otter. 'She's a female from West Africa, about eight months old, and her name is Edal. We're trying to find a good home for her in Britain but it's very difficult.' By this time we were sitting on the stairs in front of the hotel and Edal's nose was pressing against my neck. I knew that feeling so well.

Edal belonged to Mr and Mrs Malcolm Macdonald from Torridon. They came to the village that afternoon only to help two foreign girls who wanted to catch the boat to Skye. I came to the village only to meet my friend off the train. For us to meet like this was the greatest good luck ever. This was how, ten days later, Edal became mine. Now there was once again an otter at Camusfeàrna.

♦

I will now give some of the information that Malcolm Macdonald wrote down for me about Edal's early life.

'We were living in Nigeria near the town of Sapele. We both love animals and the house was full of them. One day my wife Paula went to the market and found a man who was selling two baby otters, a male and a female. She bought the female and we named her Edal. She was only three or four weeks old and we had to feed her with warm milk in a baby's bottle. We didn't know much about African otters then, only that they are bigger than British ones: more than one and a half metres long and very strong. The nights were quite cold, so Edal slept in our bed at first, then in a box full of newspapers in a corner of our bedroom. She loved to lie on her back, holding a bottle of milk and drinking it happily. Edal soon learned to use the garden for her toilet needs. The first time we put her in a bath, she was afraid of the water and cried. Every day we made the water deeper and soon she loved swimming in the bath and playing with different plastic birds and animals. Her usual cry was a high 'Whee' sound but she had other different cries also. She learned to climb the stairs to our bedroom and liked to sleep in the bathroom during the day, lying on a towel. She loved to play with our cats, and our dog Priscilla looked after her like a mother. After some time she began to eat fresh fish and we also gave her eggs and butter. We went for evening walks with her and the dog and the two cats. She was afraid of strangers but felt safe when she was with us. When she felt safe, she was loving and playful and liked to be with people.

The time came for us to go back to Britain for a holiday. We didn't want to leave Edal with another family because she was still very young and became unhappy if we were away for too long. We decided to take her with us to Britain and find a good home for her there, if possible. The journey back to London was really terrible for Edal. The aeroplane from Benin to Lagos was very hot, like an oven. In Lagos we gave her cold baths and iced water to drink. When we finally got to London she was weak, hungry and terribly tired but we still had to travel by train to Inverness.

Here in Scotland her health began to get better. She eats well and has grown a lot. Since she left Nigeria, she has put on five kilos and she's very strong. We often take her to the beach and show her where to find fish in the rock pools. One day we were driving along and stopped to pick up two young tourists who wanted to catch the boat for Skye. That's why we stopped at Kyle of Lochalsh and why we were walking past the hotel when you came and spoke to us. What a piece of luck!'

Chapter 10   Edal's New Home

We didn't decide anything on the day when we first met. The Macdonalds naturally wanted to get to know me better and to

Edal having a meal

Edal playing with glass balls

see my home. They promised to write to me. Then Edal jumped into the car and they drove away. A week later they brought Edal to Camusfeàrna for an afternoon. A few days after that, Malcolm and Paula came to spend the weekend, planning to leave Edal with me when they left.

In the days before they arrived, Jimmy Watt and I were very busy. I didn't want to repeat any of the mistakes that I made with Mij. I sent Malcolm Macdonald one of Mij's leather harnesses for Edal to wear. With Jimmy's help, I closed in part of the field near the house and made a swimming pool in it. We brought water from the stream to fill the pool. I didn't think that Edal needed to stay shut in for long but I didn't want her to run away.

On the third day of their visit, while Edal was asleep on the sofa, Paula and Malcolm left silently. They were very sad and I understood perfectly how they felt: it was like losing a child. Jimmy and I sat waiting for Edal to wake up. Soon Morag arrived to help us. But when Edal finally woke, she seemed quite calm. Her towel and playthings were on the floor and one of Paula's jackets lay next to her on the sofa. She began to play quite happily with Morag.

It's time to describe Edal more fully. Her hands are a beautiful shape, much more like a person's hands than Mijbil's were. She uses them for eating, cleaning her teeth and playing with her glass balls, matches or pens. She lies on her back and changes things from one hand to the other, and sometimes to her feet also. She loves to hide her playthings inside a box or a shoe – even a shoe with a foot inside it. She likes to steal things out of visitors' pockets while they're sitting. Then she hurries away with the things that she's found. Like Mij, she loves playing football and pushes a ball round the room for half an hour at a time, sometimes using her tail if the ball gets too far away.

Because she grew up with people instead of her natural

Edal on the sofa

mother, there are some things she can't do well. It's difficult for her to drink milk from a dish but she drinks beautifully from a spoon. When she goes swimming, she doesn't like to go into very deep water and always stays where her feet can touch the bottom. She's a wonderful swimmer and can turn round in the water very quickly. She never bites people. If she's afraid, she just runs to a person with whom she feels safe.

Edal did in fact run away twice, each time to see Morag at Druimfiaclach. The second time Jimmy caught her half-way to the MacKinnons' house and carried her home round his neck. After two weeks there was no more danger of her escaping: she had too many interesting things to do and games to play at Camusfeàrna. Like most animals, she likes to do the same things at the same time every day. First comes her breakfast of eels from the eel-box in the stream. Then Jimmy or I take her for a two-hour walk along the coast or over the hills. During these walks she prefers to stay near us. We carry her lead with us because dogs are one of the dangers. Edal loves dogs and always wants to play with them. She doesn't know that some people in the Highlands teach their dogs to kill any otters that they see. By the end of June, Edal learned to catch fish and to swim really fast under water but she still doesn't like those parts where the sea is really deep. She mostly eats eels but I also give her butter and biscuits and other food.

Edal isn't the only new animal at Camusfeàrna this summer. Years ago, when I lived at Monreith, I kept a lot of wild geese. I gave most of them to a bird park but a few pairs were left. I sent for five young birds which were still too young to fly. They are now living happily at Camusfeàrna. We give them food and we've built a house for them to sleep in at night. This keeps them safe from foxes. Jimmy Watt and I have had to teach the young geese how to fly. Jimmy ran in front of them, waving his arms, and the geese followed him, trying to do the same. After a number of

On the beach: Jimmy Watt and the geese

crashes, they finally got the idea. A week later they could all fly
beautifully and they often go off together to beaches along the
coast.

I remember one day going with Edal to one of the white
beaches on the islands, where some visitors from a sailing boat
were having a swim. As we were talking, I saw half a mile away
my five geese. I called out to them as they went over our heads
and they turned and came down to land on the beach at our feet.
What a wonderful feeling it is to call down birds out of the sky!

In September, we went out in the boat to catch fish. Edal
swam next to the boat and sometimes climbed into it. It was
almost like having Mijbil back again. Even the geese came
swimming along with us. The dark blue sea and the white waves
breaking on the rocks, the autumn colours on land and the light
blue far-away mountains: these are the things that make
Camusfeàrna so unforgettable to me.

♦

It's October and I've been back at Camusfeàrna for six months now. I can hear the call of the deer on the hills of Skye across the water. Yesterday the wild swans were flying south over the grey sea. The stream is full of fallen leaves and more leaves are blowing along the beach in the wind. The summer of wild roses and calm blue seas is over; the short days and long nights of winter will soon be here. The waterfall will make a louder noise and the cold salty wind will push at the windows and scream round the roof. This year I'll not be here to see and hear these things. I have people to see and places to visit. But when my work in the south is finished, I'll come back again to Camusfeàrna, to the place and the animals that I love.

ACTIVITIES

Chapters 1–4

Before you read

1 You need to know some of the animals, birds and fish which come in the story. Use a dictionary. Find the right number of the picture for each of the words below and write the name and number together, e. g. *1 a goat.*

an otter	a frog
a goose	a cow
a swan	a mackerel
a goat	a deer
an eel	a fox

2 These words all come in this part of the story. Make sure that you

know them. Find the best meaning for each word.

air   alone   companion   poisonous   rocks
stream   tail   waterfall   waves

a like a river but smaller
b very big stones
c without any other people
d dangerous to eat or drink
e the part of a stream where the water falls to a lower place
f movements of the sea
g birds and animals have one but people don't
h the wind is made of this
i somebody to talk to and spend time with

After you read

3 a The writer does some very different jobs before he goes to live
      at Camusfeàrna. What are they?
   b Who is Jonnie? Why is he important to Maxwell?
   c 'She's dead.' (page 13) Who is 'she'? Why does she die?
4 Would you like to live at Camusfeàrna? Talk with other students
   about the good things and the bad things of living there. Then decide.

Chapters 5–7

Before you read

5 Read again the last sentence in Chapter 4. Maxwell says
   'Chahala's dying . . . was a beginning.' What does he mean? (The
   pictures for these chapters will help you to guess.)
6 These words come in this part of the story. Use a dictionary to
   check their meaning.
   bedclothes   footprints   gloves   harness   lead   tear
   Find the best meaning for each word:
   a To break or cut clothes, paper etc.
   b A kind of jacket made of thin pieces of skin, worn by horses.
   c These keep your hands warm.
   d These keep you warm in bed.
   e We use this to take a dog for a walk.
   f Our feet make these marks on soft ground.

After you read

7 Why is the journey from Basra to London so difficult for Gavin Maxwell? Describe three of the difficulties.

8 Tell how and why Mijbil bites Maxwell.

Chapters 8–10

Before you read

9 Talk about the problems which Gavin Maxwell has in looking after Mij. Is it a good idea to take wild animals into your home, as Maxwell does? Say why or why not.

After you read

10 At the end of Chapter 9 Maxwell writes: 'For us to meet like this was the greatest good luck ever.' Who does he meet and why does he feel so lucky?

11 Edal is one of the new arrivals at Camusfeàrna that summer. Who are the others and where do they come from?

Writing

12 During the plane journey from Basra to London the young woman on the plane was very kind and helpful. Put yourself in Gavin Maxwell's place and write a letter, thanking her for her help. Begin your letter: *Dear Friend . . .*

13 You are a visitor to Camusfeàrna and you find Mijbil very interesting. You decide to write down all the things that Mijbil does during one day. Look back at Chapter 7 for useful information. Begin like this: *08:20 a.m. Mij woke up.*

14 A friend has agreed to look after your pet dog or cat. Write notes for your friend, telling him or her what to do (food, exercise, house rules, etc.).

15 You are Edal. Write about the people in your life at Camusfeàrna: Gavin, Jimmy Watt and Morag.

Answers for the activities in this book are available from your local Pearson Education office or contact: Penguin Readers Marketing Department, Pearson Education, Edinburgh Gate, Harlow, Essex, CM20 2JE.